GOD
IS KILLING ME

PATRICK B. PARKER

PAGE PUBLISHING, INC.
Conneaut Lake, PA

First originally published by Page Publishing 2021

ISBN 978-1-6624-2292-8 (pbk)
ISBN 978-1-6624-2293-5 (digital)

Printed in the United States of America

The birthing of this book is dedicated to my wife, Kerisha High-Parker.

You have not only been the love of my life, but also my guide, my cheerleader, my biggest critic, my greatest motivator, my moral compass, my focus of inspiration, and the voice of GOD I heard when I couldn't hear anything else.

You never wavered in your encouragement; your passion is unfeigned, and your words are always genuinely from the heart.

Your faithfulness is unequalled, and your patience is unmatched by any one whom I have ever known. You have always desired the best for me and made me better in every area of my life. You have undoubtedly made my experience in this life a greater one.

Not many souls on this earth would endure the trials and tribulations we have encountered, and yet still display the agape love you have to cover my fallibility and uphold me, even when I couldn't uphold myself. Your character, dedication, and strength are truly a testament that will be accounted worthy in the presence of our Almighty Creator. I am honored to have been chosen to be the man GOD has placed as protector of your life; I continue to hope that our future will include additional months, weeks, and years of added grace to display the beauty of what marriage and love should be to those who we already know and to others we will encounter. With all that I have and can give, I truly love you.

Family members, friends, and people who inspire me deserve honorable mention: my parents, Richard and Juanita Parker; my brothers, Percinio and Rick; my sister Pamela; my great uncle Bishop T. T. Terry; and my grandmothers, the late Mary Ella Barnes and the late Clotiel Greer; all of my children Travante, Kyree, and my baby girl Azaria; and I must not forget the man who has had an impact on me, and my desire to be great. I have come to love, admire, and greatly respect Mr. James D. Lacy. Thank you all for providing me with the fortitude to continue to press toward greatness in unique ways. You have all added to my desire and inspiration to "finish the work." I love all of you and owe each of you a debt of gratitude.

To all of you who helped me to form the basis of this book, thank you! These individuals either added value or detracted from my experience, but nevertheless, without them my life would have undoubtedly taken a different path. All of my pastors and brothers and sisters in Christ who have inspired me in any capacity, thank you for considering me.

I would also like to give mention to my first childhood bully and, at the time, my nemesis, Charles Petty: the lessons I learned taught me that it was okay to fight for what mattered most. Even giving the enemy little glimpses of weaknesses can provoke him to continue to try to intimidate you. Thanks to you, I don't intimidate easily.

I also want to acknowledge my childhood babysitter, whose name I won't mention. Before I was of school age, I suffered abuses that I probably compartmentalized in the recesses of my mind, and to this day I have confided my experiences only to my wife. Your actions did not destroy me; they gave me fuel to fight and a reason to share my story.

The reason I wanted to include you in the dedication is to let you know I forgive you.

I truly thank GOD for the many people I've met throughout my life and paths I've taken. These people and paths have forged my experiences and solidified my direction; I have compassion and a deep desire to not only educate but continue to be a lifelong student of the WORD of GOD, as I learn of him and seek more to decrease in my own intellectual knowledge.

Furthermore, I must acknowledge my time and experience in the United States Air Force in 1988. It was during this time that I truly learned how to pray, be humble, and exercise my faith. My physical abilities and my fortitude were tested, and I learned how resilient I could be, as well as how relentless I would become. For all of these life lessons, I am thankful.

CONTENTS

FOREWORD

WHEN EVANGELIST PATRICK Parker asked me to pen the foreword for this book, I was overcome with emotion as well as gratitude, as it shows the depth of respect and love that our brotherhood/friendship of nearly twenty years has grown. I am not only grateful for this opportunity but also both humbled and honored, as the contents of this are, simply put, many believers' life stories. Parker (as we call him) and I met in the most amazing way.

Our wives are best friends; in fact, my wife asked his wife to be in our wedding. Although Parker and I had never seen each other, we had previously spoken by phone many times, and our conversations were always about the awesomeness of Jesus! Because Parker and his wife, mother-in-law, and son arrived only the night before our wedding day, our wedding day was the first time I met him. Let me tell you—it was a God moment!

I was standing by the trunk of my car in the church parking lot when they drove up. Both he and I (not saying a word) looked up at the same time, in the same direction, not knowing, but knowing. We ran toward each other and embraced as if we had not seen each other in decades but had known each other for years! We and everyone around us knew by that experience that God was creating something special between us, a true brotherhood.

As our relationship continued to grow, we began to notice similarities in our youthful days and in our lives now.

Patrick Parker—husband, father, grandfather, evangelist, pastor, motivator, mentor, teacher, friend, son, brother—these are things he does not take for granted as he has come to realize the true meaning of a wealthy life. He is a man of great character, integrity, compassion, and love with an insatiable desire to share the gospel of Jesus Christ and help bring understanding of scripture so that we may have life and not merely exist.

Every chapter in this book is rich with content from the pages of his life or the experiences both of his own and of those close to him. For example, chapter one is appropriately titled "God Makes Prototypes, Not Stereotypes."

Being a student of the Word, Patrick's thirst and hunger for truth and understanding has led him to have many different experiences and guided him to diverse places and in the presence of people with whom new relationships form.

Gifted, born again, and believing that the world has reached a turning point, Patrick believes it is time to start sharing with everyone some simple basic truths, and those truths are in the pages of this book.

He knows that if God can make him "a new creation," he can do it for anyone. This book, in short, is about hope, joy, triumph, resurrection, and the power to make a difference and become something or someone other than a stereotype; it's about becoming the man or woman who is a believer in life, happiness, joy, peace, kindness, humbleness, love, and meekness.

"You better tell somebody" is what my brother and friend is known for saying, and this book holds true to that; he is telling somebody, anybody, and everybody who would hear of the experiences of his "secret journey" what he has learned and what he has come to understand.

This is a man who has experienced the mercies and the grace of God, and wants to share with the believer and nonbeliever alike. God has to kill the "you" that the world has created to make the "new you."

My prayer is that you will enjoy his story as much as I enjoy the experience of having a brother in my life whom God uses to express the gospel and his love for you.

Pastor Leslie C. Haymon

Chronicles of Dying to the Flesh

PEOPLE WHO STRUGGLE with their faith often need to know what relationship is and why we should embrace a personal relationship with our Savior, the Creator of all, GOD. What they understand about their spirituality as they begin their life's journey and grow in faith increases or decreases based on their experiential relationship with GOD.

This I know: our faith is provoked *or* adversely antagonized based on our life experiences. According to the word of GOD, to every man is given a measure of faith (Eph. 4:7).

How that word or that measure of faith is activated determines whether it grows or diminishes.

Like many people, I learned faithfulness by watching those around me. I saw what might appear to some as miraculous, zealous, provocative, and the like and experienced the mundane, bewildering, hopeless, and worldliness common in the average nonbeliever's life.

In the 1970s, 60 percent of US citizens identified themselves as Christians or believers.

Four decades later, we have seen this number increase only a mere 17 percent! For those of you keeping record, that means today only 77 percent of Americans identify as Christians. How can this be when we can reach the uttermost parts of the world through sharing the gospel via modern technology, social media, evangelism, TV, and radio? This information may surprise some, but others know it is the norm. Modern technology has changed our lives. Why haven't more people become believers? Why haven't we seen a significant increase in the number of believers across the world? These are questions I aim to answer in this book.

My second aim is to provoke understanding in you, my reader. I pray God awakes your spirit man to realize that we are not here because of our own accord, nor because of some "evolutionary phenomena." The Creator meticulously gave each of us a destiny, a promise, an assignment, a journey, and unique gifts when we were born.

Remarkably, he implanted all of it within a seed. That seed he released contained the *pneuma*, or the breath of GOD. To receive this breath, each one of us must be willing to give up our own identity.

The Most High desires to have a relationship with each of his children. Unfortunately, many people who claim to know who he is don't fully recognize that even the Bible says two gods claim to rule in this world. The first is Satan, who deceives us with lies, ritualism, lawlessness, vanity, confusion, fear, and manipulation. His tactics represent the seven deadly sins: lust, gluttony, greed, sloth, wrath, envy, and pride. The second is the GOD of all creation—ABBA Father, who is the I AM, AHAYAH ASHER AHAYAH, the Ancient of Days, who in his infinite wisdom created all things (Isa. 54:16)—who allows us to grow in grace of the seven spirits of GOD: Spirit of the LORD, Spirit of wisdom, Spirit of understanding, Spirit of counsel, Spirit of power, Spirit of knowledge, and Spirit of the fear of the Lord. Here's the catch: Only through the life of Christ as the door can we find the way, the truth, and the life (John 14:6).

I thank Almighty God for giving me the inspiration to bring these thoughts and ideas to life, giving you a perspective to how a man first sees the world and then relates his experience to his spirituality.

I am not writing this book to establish my expertise. Instead, I pray that you find profound insight into how you undertake your journey and that you encourage others to strengthen their relationship and their faith. I hope these words inspire you to share this book with others as you gain insight, wisdom, understanding, and peace from my personal disclosure and testimony.

I hope to share with you my journey, my understanding, and my point of view—not based on religion but on building a solid foundation of relationship with the Most High GOD.

I pray you find the answers you are seeking in these seven chapters. I will disclose some life lessons that I've learned through my transparency and revelation of GOD's relevance to our existence; may the God of hope fill you with all joy because you have taken time to read this book. Be blessed, be empowered, and be encouraged.

CHAPTER 1

God Makes Prototypes, Not Stereotypes

How do you pass the diamond test?

The way to test a diamond is to heat it as hot as possible and then allow it to cool rapidly (quench it). Heat won't damage a real diamond, but it will shatter an imitation diamond through the pressure of extreme heating and cooling.

I spent years trying to emulate others until I had an epiphany: GOD has wonderfully and fearfully created me in his own image. I'm uniquely one of a kind, and GOD has the patent on my life.

In Genesis, we find GOD has laid a foundational example of what he ordained for us from the beginning.

Examples of GOD's redemptive love are everywhere. In fact, one of the most paradigmatic examples we see is found in Genesis 3:15, which speaks about the enmity between flesh and spirit, which all human beings endure.

Our flesh continually desires what is contrary to what the spirit desires; we are all vulnerable to this enduring battle. Because of this, we must mortify the members of the flesh—that is, anything which draws or holds us away from being in relationship with the Lord.

In my personal walk, I've found that the same temptations common to all men continue from generation to generation. This is precisely wise in the infinite wisdom of GOD. We all need the same salvation, which the providence of Christ foreshadows; he came through the lineage of humanity but maintained the sanctity of his divinity. The life of Christ is a prototype that no one can ever duplicate. When Christ was crucified, the veil that separated because of sin was torn asunder, allowing us to have access to GOD again through the accomplished work of Jesus Christ.

We no longer need a priest to enter the "holiest of holies" on behalf of unworthy men and women; neither do we need the blood of bullocks, goats, lambs, and turtledoves. The blood Jesus shed for us once and for all atoned for our sins, gave us access to the Father, and satisfied the penalty that he assessed against humanity.

Jesus instructed his disciples to "follow him;" this command extends to everyone who claims to be a believer in Christ. The prerequisite for us to live is that we must be willing to die.

The Apostle Paul admonishes us that "to live is Christ, and to die is gain" (Phil. 1:21). Our lives are hidden in Christ, and not until we enter his rest do we gain access to this divine life.

The gate through which we access the abundant life of Christ is engraved with the intrinsic pangs of suffering. The bible tells us it pleased GOD to bruise his own son (Isa. 53:10); because of that bruising, our iniquities are forgiven.

Suffering is a personal yet intimate way for each of us to partake in the fellowship of the life of Christ. One might equate it to having a personal key that no one else can use to enter.

In our minds, we can fathom only the love that GOD has for us; however, as we submit ourselves to GOD's plan, we find that in our lives, GOD's love often manifests as chastening.

"Whom He loves, he also chastens" (Prov. 3:12). I have concluded GOD not only gives us good gifts, but he also loves us even when we feel like he's crushing us. Our physical condition pales in comparison to our spiritual well-being. We can be assured that GOD doesn't need any stereotypes. We were made originals, and GOD alone has the blueprints to each soul which he created.

GOD IS KILLING ME

Life Lesson No. 1
"My flesh is my fear."

But I keep my body and bring it into subjection:
lest by any means, when I have preached to others, I should be a castaway. (1 Cor 9:27)

"I once was lost / but now I'm found." This popular excerpt
from one of the most recognized gospel songs in the world, "Amazing
Grace," is an adequate description of the profound love of GOD and
his meticulous detail, which he aligned to provide us with access
to Christ. GOD spared no expense in reaching out to us even while
Christ was being brutally and ruthlessly crucified. Jesus, in his compassion, asked the Father to forgive those who inflicted the ultimate
harm, which resulted in him being beaten beyond recognition.

As we are found in our sin, we are unrecognizable to GOD. Why?
GOD does not associate with that nature or the phenomena of sin that
causes us to be hidden from his presence because of his holiness.

For us to be in relationship with GOD, we must be willing to
"uncloak" our lives by bearing our infirmities and faults. It requires
us to break away from the flesh and be revealed in the light of GOD
on the other side; this is done by beating our flesh into submission,
even unto death.

I consider myself an avid student of words, and seek to know
and understand etymological definitions as well. Words that appears
to have universal meanings often do not translate into the words one
might think; when it comes to understanding and determining the
origin of certain words and their relevance to the text, the meaning
changes. How fascinating!

The more we draw nigh to GOD, the less our natural world or
language makes sense, just as the natural world is converse to the
spiritual world.

In our English language, the word *phobia* means anything
pertaining to fear that is extreme, or irrational—that is, abnormal.
Phobias are often phenomena that cause people to avoid various
behaviors and conditions or things.

Ironically, the definition for the *fear of* GOD does not rationally fit within the context of a definitive nature; thus, it can't logically be defined as a phobia. The fear of GOD, called *taqwa*, is an Islamic term that means fear of Allah; the closest in definition is a place in one's spirit between fear and love, which draws one closer to being fearless and full of faith.

We are commanded to fear GOD and keep his commandments as we are made aware that the fear of the LORD is the beginning of wisdom and knowledge (Prov. 9:10, Prov. 1–9, and Prov. 9–7).

We are in a constant battle to either resist or succumb to the desires of the flesh. These are situations we face daily—our eating habits, our desires to do as we please or what satisfies our needs or carnal nature, desires to enjoy pleasure or experience various pleasures or luxuries, and even our desires to covet others' possessions, properties, or people in their lives.

Because our desires are ingrained into our inner psyche, we don't recognize the temptations. We have developed either a spiritual defense or a natural tolerance, which bypasses our physiological governing system, similar to how secondhand smoke enters our lungs.

When you are attacked, do you recognize that in that moment you have an opportunity to stand against those forces and can choose to actively resist them? GOD is pleased when we acknowledge our problems and stand fearless or share our weaknesses openly through confession and declaration.

In these acts of transparency, we learn to resist temptation and build confidence in the truth that GOD will help us, cover us, and provide a way for us to escape.

These phenomena are introduced to us at birth through how we socialize and how the world defines our value. During our developmental stages, whatever we believe is most valuable inevitably affects the value we place on ideals.

One of the hardest things to do is to reprogram our minds to displace a value we have fixed in our lives. The Bible calls these things idols. Many examples of idols are mentioned, which represent things that men have valued or honored more than relationship with the one true GOD.

The same phenomena exist today. One of our greatest addictions, passions, pastimes, and hobbies includes sharing our lives on Facebook and Twitter. Games, video chats, social groups, status updates, and a myriad of applications allow us to vicariously share our lives with friends, family, and others across the world. Studies have been done that show how much time the average individual spends on Facebook versus meditating, in devotion, or studying GOD's word.

One of GOD's Ten Commandments is, "Thou shalt have no other gods before me" (Exo. 20:2). Anytime a thing, concept, person, or idea preoccupies one's life or dominates one's time, the thing in question has become a god in that individual's life. When we allow a thing to become lord over our lives, it influences our actions, our thoughts, our behavior, and often our beliefs. As we learn to submit to the will of GOD for our lives, we will find that often the things which used to be difficult to overcome are no longer challenges for us. One of the biggest issues we will encounter as we are transformed more to GOD's image is not to have any other gods before him; if any man is to believe in GOD, he must first believe that he is GOD. Believing GOD builds our faith; our hope of life eternal grows.

This hope is the substance upon which to build our expectations in the Word of GOD. Consequently, this hope is also the foundation upon which every believer asserts his trust that we will live again. The foundation of this faith is grounded and rooted in the life, death, burial, and resurrection of Jesus Christ. To understand this, one must believe that death does not have the final say over us once we accept Christ as our Lord and Savior. The exchange which Jesus provides is his life (righteousness) in exchange for our death (sins).

Even though salvation is a gift from GOD, we bear a responsibility to continue sharing the gospel. Others can experience the love of Christ through our hands, hearts, mouths, and feet. When we partake of his life, which he laid down for us, we also take up his nature which he possesses and which is eternal (immortal). In exchange, we covenant with him and agree to give our lives to ensure others can share and become joint-heirs to this great salvation that Jesus Christ gives us. The lure of this is that we inherit his salvation not only in this world but in the world to come. The drawback is that receiving this inheritance requires that we pass through death to acquire life. The death we must experience is not just physical but also mental; we must also die to the cares of this world.

How difficult it is to crucify one's self! We are inherently taught that self-preservation was necessary and subconsciously desired. In this life, our own self-serving nature constantly bombards us. All of our philosophies and moral and social consciousness insist that in all things we should consider ourselves first.

This concept underlies many wayward and warped philosophies about life, condemns the idea of "the greater good," and dismisses the ideal beliefs that our lives serve a bigger purpose than we understand. For this reason, God has given us various examples of altruism in the bible. The greatest display of GOD's love is seen in Jesus's birth, life, death, and resurrection.

To experience the same level of relationship and potential, we must be willing to exchange our temporal reality for eternal immortality, which everyone who comes into sonship and becomes an heir to the legacy of Christ inherits.

Death is described as darkness, emptiness, and a place of dryness and fear; contemporaries define it as the grave, or *sheol*, the place of separation from GOD. Unless we embrace the eternal love of GOD provided in Jesus, we have no hope in death. A child of the Most High has great expectations, which transcend beyond the scope and power of death. We will continue to explore this point throughout the book.

One may ask, Why death? We will explore this important question in more detail too. An interesting quote I've read states, "A man who has not found something to die for isn't fit to live." This quote intrigues me not because it challenges me to justify what I live for, but because it charges me to establish something I'm willing to die for. "What does it profit a man to gain great possessions in this world and lose his own soul?" (Mk. 8:36)

The inevitable questions we must all answer are these: What is the cost of the exchange for earthly gain? Are we willing to pay the price?

If my life could be broken down into chapters that would be written into the pages of a book like Paul's, I should have been considered unfit to be a citizen of either Rome or the kingdom of GOD, but in the bowels of his divine mercy, we are all given opportunities to course correct.

The question that remains is, How many chapters or episodes do we get to vindicate the errors of our ways? What you will discover as you venture further into my spiritual journey depends on who is holding the pen and paper when my story is told. Here's my advice: the person who reads my notes should spend some time getting to know the author.

CHAPTER 2

To Live Is Christ; To Die Is Gain

Life Lesson No. 2
"The true tragedy of life is not that we die, but
what dies in us as we live."

SADLY, I HAVE learned that oftentimes, it takes great tragedy, trauma,
or trouble to forge what may be our finest moments, memories, or
greatest milestones. Fortunately, whatever the enemy intended for
our demise might be our deliverance.

Our Creator has always displayed his presence, authority, and
glory throughout the earth.

We, as mankind, have a defect, which we inherited because of
our forefather Adam; we have received the nature or the DNA of our
forefathers. This means we also received the same flaws and fallibility.
This nature gives us our capacity to be sinners.

It is also the reason for which we have received our terminal
nature—and why we need a Savior (one who can counteract the con-
sequence of physical and spiritual death).

The Bible tells us that sin has a price, or a wage attached to it,
and that penalty is death. On Earth, death has its characteristics;
however, if a person doesn't choose a relationship with Jesus Christ as

Lord, then the dominion of death has an even more final and fearful meaning.

Imagine life as a full glass of water—pure and refreshing. When we enter this life from birth, we inherit DNA from both of our parents, and various contaminants collect in our glass. Whether good or bad, we also inherit our parents' spiritual heritage. Our glass of water is full of natural bacteria, microorganisms, and other things we can't see (spiritually); neither can some of these things be determined until various stages or ages in our life development. Now the glass that appears to be life-giving still contains its ability to give life, but it also contains the ability to bring forth some destructive things as well. As the light shines into the water, through the glass we can see some things that we couldn't see before. As heat is applied to the water (which could represent life's trials), it becomes agitated and then begins to boil at the proper time. When the temperature reaches 212 degrees Fahrenheit, the water changes form, and the molecules separate when they rise from the glass. They transform into steam; coincidentally, when the steam cools, the properties allow the steam to condensate and become water, again fresh and refreshing (as it was intended in its original state).

This analogy is a close example of man conceived in sin and shaped in iniquity (Psa. 51:5). If we examined ourselves only from the external perspective, we appear to be perfect. However, the hidden properties of the water refer to our fallen nature and propensity to sin. As we grow and learn about God, his plan, and his Son, we have an opportunity to place our lives into the Light of the World. When we see our lives as we are, all the things that are hidden from our sight are seen, or exposed (John 1:5). The agitation refers to the power of the Holy Spirit to stir our hearts and "prick us." It is then that we turn away (repent) from our evil nature and deny ourselves. It's then that the power of love is applied as ascribed by the boiling point of life. This is the juncture when light and darkness (representing both our good and evil natures) separate, and sin is abolished. The blood covers all hidden things as we attempt to denounce the works of the flesh. The change is similar to water becoming steam and then returning to its previous state to be used for its original intent. Thus, the life of Christ restores us to God's intended state for us—as heirs and joint-heirs.

Now this water can be used to pour out to those who thirst for a right relationship with God. The latter state of this symbolic water is alive and contains only life-giving properties.

In this example, you can see how the cycle of a simple glass of water is not much different from the process a soul undergoes through Christ, given that it can develop and experience natural, spiritual, emotional, and physiological growth.

GOD monitors our growth through every phase of life. Many times, I was unaware of his presence until the moments I felt either the greatest distress or extreme peace.

I have always sensed and known that a divine presence guides my life, although if I'm honest, I ignored it for years. Throughout my formative years, I was often told my demeanor and character were "peculiar." I attributed it to my family heritage, genetics, and even my upbringing, but I was always aware of GOD's hand on my life.

CHAPTER 3

Let This Mind Be in You, Which Is Also in Christ Jesus

Life Lesson No. 3
"The mind is the rudder that controls the destiny
of your life's ship."

THE UNDERLYING STORY of the poem "Invictus" by William Ernest Henley gives us an insight into the mind of an individual who is facing death but is determined to maintain his dignity with courage despite the trials life places before us. The only way we can sustain this posture is by having the mind of Christ, which I need to govern my heart daily. Without it, I could not share my story. The end of the poem refrains, "I AM the master of my fate / I AM the captain of my soul."

One question I've always pondered is this: Where is the mind of a man found in his body?

The answer, I've concluded, is in Christ.

This is the place where you must prepare to be isolated, separated, aggravated, degraded, and even hated. After men have written you off, after God has clothed you with humility, you will be elevated. Our lives are like clay in the hands of the master potter; as we continue to conform to his hand of correction, direction, instruction, and consecration, GOD releases more of his characteristics into our weakened forms. We are molded through conforming to his word, which becomes the essential ingredient that strengthens what remains. We are daily, hourly—continually—being made into God's unchanging image. This transformation into GOD's image doesn't require our help, but demands our submission. "Not by might nor by our power, but solely and exclusively by the power of GOD's spirit" (Zech. 4:6).

After we have suffered awhile, we are then made a vessel fit for usage by the master potter. GOD is patient with his work, especially in the one who GOD has invested his treasure in. Just as one must search and unearth precious treasures like oil, gold, coal, and diamonds, we must be purged from the earth, which we have been encased in naturally and physiologically. To make this more simplistic, we as mankind are the sum of our thoughts, visions, emotions, passions, values, words, actions, and plans. Therefore, if we know the word of GOD, we give the word authority to activate GOD's power into the details of our lives. As we yield to the word, we allow the hand of GOD to correct, direct, and protect us in the finer points of our destiny. Ever wondered if GOD had his hand on your life? GOD is heavy-handed; only one hand is needed to govern our lives. When GOD uses his hands, its either creative or destructive; one hand guides and the other corrects, directs, and protects. When we see GOD's hands, they perform great tasks that are beyond man's ability to handle. Jesus commended his spirit into the hands of GOD. Our father handles us with one hand to protect us because he loves us with such a great love. His love appears to crush us, but it only brings out the best in us as we learn to yield to our trust in Him.

Now that I've written almost four chapters of this book, GOD is revealing his plan to bring this message to fruition; a new form of yielding is taking place in my life. I have always sought the approval of men, for validation, provision, or qualification. I have learned that GOD is jealous of whom we allow to receive credit or glory. When he is preparing you for your destiny, all bets are off! I no longer seek others to validate my time or efforts, and I hope this helps the person who might be in the same position to overcome waiting on others to establish your validation.

You will find yourself in positions where everything that gives your life its value will be strategically and methodically removed. Friends who said they loved you, loved ones who said they'd never leave you, and anything you depend on for balance, security, or assurance will all disappear.

As a man thinks in his heart, he sees a vision; from his vision, he develops emotions and builds his passion. Whatever he is passionate about, he establishes values for, which he affirms with words and takes action by planning to achieve his goals. Without a vision, the people perish (Prov. 29:18).

Remarkably, this is where the name for a common household device comes from: tele- (to send to/from the mind) plus vision (what is seen). The common thread that allows us to relate is that the process began in the mind of one person and was transmitted to the mind of another via an electric medium. The Word of GOD is living and powerful; it is the plan of GOD to transmit his thoughts to our minds. Ironically, the concepts of reality—that is, truth—which we perceived since birth, must be disconnected (unplugged) in order to receive the signal through the frequency of the Holy Spirit.

The medium GOD used is a familiar concept we can relate to in Jesus Christ (Son of GOD/Son of Man). The converter is the cross of Christ. The conduit is the blood of Jesus, which provides the energy for new life (life of the body is in the blood [Lev. 17:11]). The human body functions as the blood receives new life via oxygen into the system, and circulates into and through every major organ of the body. If the blood stops, medically, so does the process of life. Likewise, if we don't receive GOD's refreshing wind of the Spirit, via Jesus, we have no life in us; we die, and then we are judged.

In GOD, love is perfect. If we love GOD, then fear has no place in us. Therefore, hell has no power over a believer, because it's far away from the ones who love GOD. "There is no fear in love, but perfect love cast out fear" (1 John 4:18).

GOD longs to have all his creation realize his plan to redeem us from the curse of death. Unfortunately, many ignore, deny, renounce, and simply refuse the love of GOD, and like us, when we are rejected, we display our displeasure in various ways, including anger and jealousy. In fairness and deference to the truth of the Word, I will share what I believe is one question that most people might ask about GOD. Here it is: "If GOD is so good, why does he allow people to go to hell?" Let me first explain to you GOD's nature. According to the Word, "Every good and perfect gift is from above, the Father of Lights, in whom is no variableness, neither shadow of turning" (James 1:17).

GOD does not change or vary in who he intrinsically is. GOD is love. If love is rejected, the lover becomes sad, jealous, and eventually angry. The Word of GOD says even GOD is jealous! "For the Lord thy GOD is a jealous GOD among you lest the anger of the LORD thy GOD be kindled against thee from off the face of the earth" (Deut. 6:15).

Hell, or *sheol*, which is also called Hades, is described as the place of the dead. It was originally reserved for Satan and the fallen angels, who rebelled and rejected GOD.

Today it is more commonly known as the place where souls of those who die separate from GOD are sent until judgment at the end of time. When Christ returns to redeem the children of GOD, those who rejected him shall be judged and cast into the lake that burns with fire.

In this place called hell, all memories, emotions, feelings, fear, pain, and sin will be revisited upon the one who hasn't received the peace and love of GOD.

In addition, the inhabitants of hell are constantly tortured to make them renounce Christ and deny his deity, announcing their allegiance to Satan. This is to give you a brief image (television) of hell. However, I want to dispel what might be a common view of this from GOD's perspective.

As a believer, the first thing that we experience as the Word comes alive is a change of our mind. "Let this mind be in you which was also in Christ Jesus" (Phil. 2:5). When your mind changes, your point of view changes. GOD loves us even when we reject him, for the Bible says, "For whom the Lord loves, he chastens and whips" (Heb. 12:6).

The chastening of the LORD is not for the sake of inflicting punishment or causing one's will to be broken. GOD always seeks to bring us into reformation and draw us toward repentance through correction. Anytime punishment is administered without correction, there will be no justification. The Bible declares that GOD is just, and His grace and mercy are inseparable from his love for us.

The Word of God informs us of the characteristic of God's physiology. It tells us who he is and that we in relation to God are created in both his likeness and resembling his image. According to Heb 12:29, God is a consuming fire, but his nature of love is not altered or changed. The will of God is not that any soul should perish, but that all should come to repentance (2 Pet. 3:9). Because he is slow to anger, when his anger is kindled, his passion to bring us to repentance is as well. The omniscience, omnipresence, and omnipotence of God remain the same; he desires continual intimate fellowship with his children. Indispensably, he can't separate himself from what his nature is; those who are separated are inevitably consumed by his love to correct them in chastening, because his love had not consumed them in the flesh when he pursued them while they were sinners (Rom 5:8). I believe they are consumed by his jealousy from the rejection of his love.

This is an example of the intimacy God reveals as we pursue him through the mind of Christ.

The physiology of the body does not contain a physical organ called the mind, but we all know that the process of thought is formed first in the mind. The Bible says that the mind is found in the heart; we can conclude that the mind is connected to the seat of the soul and the spirit. The mind must be shielded and guarded from corruption and fear as well as negative emotions. Therefore, we can declare, "Oh grave where is your victory?" (1 Cor. 15:55–57) That is why we need the Word of GOD and the mind of Christ, which overrides our carnal mind and natural desire to operate from fear in our own desires or imaginations.

CHAPTER 4

Wait on the Lord; Again I Say Wait

Life Lesson No. 4
"The most important thing I can do is know my own weaknesses; the enemy does."

When a spy studies for his mission, he or she spends meticulous time researching how to best approach, access, attack, and annihilate the target. When the attack comes, it's sudden, unexpected, and often overwhelming, giving the perpetrator an almost assured, swift, and nearly problem-free opportunity to quickly overtake his victim with minimal effort. (*The Art of War* by Sunzi)

ALLOWING THINGS TO develop the way that GOD has designed should be our goal; let patience have its perfect work in us. "Trials work patience, patience bring forth experience, experience gives us hope, and hope makes us not ashamed" (Rom. 5:3–5). This is the process which we all undergo; however, how we handle the process is what determines how we perceive the outcome. GOD, likewise, provides each believer an opportunity to endure various trials in his own life, to bring forth the "perfect work" in us. This is achieved by developing godly patience. In my own life, this process continues daily as I face many of my greatest fears. As I realize the infallible love of GOD, I receive the revelation of his plan for my life. The perfect work of GOD peels you from your comfort zones, and leaves you uncovered and feeling forsaken and unsure in your situation. Meanwhile, GOD, through the divine plan which he has orchestrated, is evolving into, through, and around our lives. Trials are external; they will come into everyone's life. Experiences are intrinsic phenomena and uniquely different for each person based upon who they are, where they're from, and what issues in life they are given to overcome.

I believe this is how GOD has predetermined our purpose and strategically positioned each of us to be overcomers. Experiences are worked through our lives. Hope, although internal, is built up daily, hourly, year by year. As we increase in hope, we gain more confidence in our ability, in our future, and in our purpose.

This resolution of destiny grows around us. We build confidence not in ourselves but in GOD to finish what he has begun in us.

Losing a loved one, a traumatic event that alters one's destiny, family issues/crises, wars, severe circumstances such as job or home loss, or any traumatic change may be a catalyst to our immediate encounter with who GOD is or shall become in our lives.

Anytime our hope is deferred, challenged, or grows dim, therein is the place and opportunity when GOD will intervene and intercede in the affairs of men's lives. The intervention GOD performs separates us from our past, incubates us in our present, and prepares us for our future.

This phenomenon is demonstrated in nature and throughout the Bible. The caterpillar in its primary form experiences a period of hibernation, and then a period when it spins its cocoon around itself; it creates an incubation in which it begins to change into a butterfly. As a butterfly, it elevates from its former existence to assume its new identity as a new creature. The same can be said for Abram in Genesis. First GOD instructed him to leave his dwelling (separation). Abram leaves Sodom with Lot, and then makes a covenant with GOD. GOD blessed Abram and his seed (incubation); afterward, GOD gave Abram a new name, Abraham, and his wife who was barren was also renamed from Sarai to Sarah. Abraham was given a new title and status too (elevation). He is now and forever known as the father of faith. The former life of Abram was forever altered and, subsequently, the future destiny his legacy for all time.

Whenever GOD intersects any individual's life and breathes the *ruach*, or "breath of life," over one's destiny, an intrinsic change happens and affects not only the individual's life immediately, but also engages the destiny of all future generations forever. The prerequisite for this level of intervention is activated as we learn to exhibit patience and obedience to adhere to the will of GOD in our lives. This has been an area in my own life where I found my personal struggles have risen more frequently. I am consciously aware of the places in my own life where I find it increasingly difficult for me to allow GOD, day by day, to separate, incubate, and then elevate me. However, like the Apostle Paul, I must allow myself to die daily, crucifying my flesh to the elements which control my flesh and my emotions; whatever I am unable to reconcile, I continually lift these issues to the Lord, knowing the great sufficiency of his grace.

The greatest struggle in our lives is letting go. As children, we are taught and trained to be selfish; GOD requires us to be selfless. Our human nature is immersed in a sin culture. One cliché spoken the most in this society is "Self-preservation is the first law of nature." This statement implies we have an innate desire to preserve our own existence at the expense of all others. This creates a hierarchy of "survival of the fittest" mentality, which has permeated our psyche.

Spiritually, we apply the same defensive mechanisms toward GOD's intervention, even if his ultimate desire is to elevate us to a blessed place. Unfortunately, we futilely resist what clearly is a process of how he chastens who he loves.

To be transparent, I admit patience has never been my strong suit. Many years of my younger life as a Christian, I battled with letting patience be perfected in my life and was often torn between what I knew regarding the promises of GOD and my present experiences.

I experienced some of my greatest challenges with finances. I never felt destitute or "broke," but at times I wasn't as financially successful as I thought deserved to be through hard work. The truth was that I did not trust GOD's plan for increase in my life. I had to take a deeper look at my spiritual giving, tithing, and stewardship of GOD's resources he had provided to me. I concluded that I wasn't adequately sowing the seeds of time into my gifting as well as my level of tithing into the kingdom principle of giving. When I decided to trust GOD with my finances, my life became more fulfilling. I could see increase in how we received blessings and favor by my faith in the Word of GOD growing as a principle of my belief to trust GOD.

Just before preparing to write the fifth chapter of this book, I lost my grandmother, the greatest believer I had the privilege and honor of knowing.

Through her, I experienced firsthand genuine agape love, unequaled zeal, and undying faith in the Word of GOD. She had a remarkable temperance, unmatched patience, and a wealth of wisdom she willingly shared with every soul she encountered. Even as a child, I witnessed the great love she had for Jesus.

Remarkably, my encounters with her are what I believe in time has inspired and influenced my pursuit of ministry.

My greatest hope is that I can carry on the legacy of being at least as influential and genuine in the lives of others as she has been in mine.

Thus, in my pursuit, I am relentlessly striving to acquire the type of relationship with the Creator that will make my grandmother and our Savior Jesus Christ proud at the end of my life's journey. For this irrepressible time in my life, I am eternally grateful that GOD provided me with such a great mentor who lived to a full life of ninety-three years.

Job well done, Big Mamma!

CHAPTER 5

Unless a Seed Falleth to the Ground and Dies, It Cannot Bring Forth Fruit

Life Lesson No. 5
"Everyone wants to go to heaven, but nobody wants to die."

IN THE GARDEN of Gethsemane, we witnessed Jesus as a human being; he exhibits his humanity when crying out to the Father. He knew his impending fate—crucifixion of his flesh. At first, Jesus was reluctant to accept GOD's plan, but after he prayed, Christ submitted to the will of GOD, which was to hang and die on the cross for our sins. Obedience does not always have self at the center of its agenda, especially if the outcome can benefit others.

Doing what is right at the cost of your own peril to ensure others' well-being is the definition of sacrifice.

The last enemy that GOD will destroy is death; it will be swallowed by the same pit where it stands as the gatekeeper of the lost souls, and death shall be no more (Rev. 21:4).

Death is as much a part of life as the breath we breathe. To many, it represents finality, but to believers, it's only a gate we may pass through to go into GOD's realm, which is cloaked by the flesh and humanity. Naturally, our flesh fears what we can't control. Although we physiologically understand the process, we still wrestle with understanding what we will experience after we take our last breath.

This is our hope. GOD has not given us a spirit of fear (2 Tim. 1:7).

Fear is the antithesis of love. GOD *is* love. Without the anchor of love, we cannot navigate through eternity to GOD. Jesus provides us with the road map engraved in his flesh, offers us a doorway through death, and gives us the key to the door—the Word of GOD.

In the last chapter, we talked about patience and time. In everyone's life, death interrupts time and thrusts us into another reality where we experience the unknown. We do this either without an anchored hope and not rooted in faith, or based on love, where we accept GOD's plan of redemption and are assured that an eternal destiny in heaven exists. I am not implying that anyone must agree, nor will I attempt to sway your belief. However, I am confident that each one of us will intersect with the reality of death, unless Christ returns first.

In nature, we can perform scientific experiments that show the death process, from which we can definitively identify that out of death comes forth life.

From these observations, I can reasonably assume that we will also experience another dimension of life-consciousness after we meet our demise on earth. The Bible clearly states as long as the earth remains, there will be seed time and harvest (Gen. 8:22).

This passage is saying that after the flesh returns to the earth, it will be harvested again. How we invested our time here on earth will determine how we will be remembered. Death has been a primary focus of society for centuries. People who lived during certain time periods thought considerably about and contemplated death and dying. Mortality is our dressing room; it's where we eventually outgrow our finite capacity and take on infinite capacity, where we will be united with the source of all life and power. GOD is that eternal source from whence all derives.

While we are here in this earth-season, we must put on immortality and prepare to coexist with GOD in eternity. I have come to believe it's nearly impossible to not challenge one's spiritual intellect to explore GOD's plan as the architect of the universe. It behooves us to know or at least pursue the knowledge that is rooted and grounded in the familiar concept of love.

Consider the concept of farming, which applies the principle of reaping and sowing; this commonsense approach shows that it requires patience, time, and sacrifice to produce a harvest.

First, the farmer must invest in plowing and sowing into the land.

Farmers work predominantly during the daytime and rest at night. Interestingly enough, farmers plant their seeds eight inches apart; every eight inches represents a beginning. Although the farmer is not guaranteed a harvest, every year, he continues in faith to work the land and tend the livestock. Each principle the farmer applies comes from the Bible; after he has waited for a season, he receives a yield from the land.

Likewise, GOD's concepts teach us to work while it's day, sow the land, invest in seed, till the ground, water our seed frequently, be patient, and, over time, expect a harvest. The yield of our harvest depends on how we till the ground.

As a man who believes GOD strengthens our character with each experience we go through, I have become acutely aware that learning to endure various trials and hardships in life prepares us to experience things that may arise later. That time will be when GOD determines it is necessary to develop us or cause us to overcome issues he foresees may arise.

In return, we learn patience and how to trust what we experience, because GOD will, through diverse methods, sustain us and preserve us. What he does will prepare us for a destiny that intrinsically interweaves us into his omniscient plan.

Many alliterations throughout the Bible reference or mention reaping, sowing, or ideas related to farming and harvesting.

GOD has positioned us as gardeners and care keepers. Cain and Abel provided our first example of the requirement GOD has when requesting an offering. In the story, Cain offered tainted fruit, which had fallen to the ground. Abel offered GOD the best of the flock, which he painstakingly raised; he ensured that he presented the first of the harvest and the best of his flock to GOD.

Likewise, GOD honors every seed we present to him, but our presentation makes the difference. After it is presented, GOD glorifies it, multiplies it, and then edifies it, as it relates to the needs in our lives.

Furthermore, we learn to exemplify giving as a way of life and not just a vain tradition.

Even in death, GOD finds a way to give; through Jesus' death we gained eternal life.

Through experiencing trials, we gain patience; through troubles, we gain hope and a future expectation of the glory of GOD. I know that the most overwhelming experiences of my life are preparing me to make more room to receive GOD's greatest favor in the latter days of my life.

The most frustrating thing I believe can occur and possibly hinder one's spiritual growth is one's ability to discipline himself while waiting on GOD to expound his glory tangibly. GOD dwells in the realm of the invisible. In our three-dimensional existence, we are not fully aware of the workings of the Spirit.

The Bible clearly states our eyes have not seen, nor ears heard, the things that GOD has prepared for us (1 Cor. 2:9). Through this passage of scripture, we discover GOD's workings are not designed to entertain us from the natural perspective. We cannot fully know the plans of GOD nor his objectives for our lives. However, we have the Word of GOD as a road map and prayer as a medium. Prayer acts as our compass to activate our patience while we await GOD's will being fulfilled. For new believers especially, great patience is required. I'm reminded of the process of planting a tree. After the seed is planted, the gestation period starts. During that period, no activity takes place. After it rains, the seed undergoes a metamorphosis and breaks open. That first process allows the sprouts to grow down further into the ground, where the seed was planted. No visible evidence indicates a tree is there, but under the surface, the roots are forming and strengthening to stabilize and reinforce what will be a tree.

In Jerusalem, this same process occurs in the olive groves. The unique difference is that the roots are so strong they begin to break into the bedrock and intertwine into the solid rock located underneath the surface.

The message here is both natural and spiritual. GOD's Word is spirit and truth. It's internalized, where it takes hold and is strengthened; then it springs forth, and it is not easily moved once it's established. Jesus's life reflects this process.

Jesus became the firstborn from the dead of GOD for all mankind; he was born, rooted in love, established in truth, crucified for humanity, buried in victory, and resurrected into eternity. I don't think we can escape it: we've been internally programmed with a thirst and a longing for the creator, even though many of us still deny his very existence.

Mankind has sought out a plethora of methods to discover who, how, and why we are here. Many men—from young to old—have quested for knowledge about this and consistently pursued philosophical, mental, and spiritual answers, but JEHOVAH GOD has been the common thread throughout time.

Our common denominator that connects us and keeps us is the life and person of Jesus Christ. He provides a common thread with an uncommon solution of sacrificial love. Christ's life was the catalyst to reunite us to him in right-standing relationship, and it gave us a right to live eternally in GOD's kingdom. By contrast, we are bombarded with opposing forces meant to distract, distress, and destroy our faith in GOD. Situations may cause us to become hopeless, live loveless, and conform to this world.

As a result, we become helpless as we walk through life without faith. We begin to act mindlessly and ultimately adopt godless ways.

Even though I have been in ministry for the past twenty-three years, I admit that at various times I have found myself in many, if not all, of these states. Thus, we have been instructed by the Apostle Paul to crucify the mind of the flesh daily, because as we go through life, an infinite number of things have the potential to influence us.

To allow our minds to die to the things which motivate, stimulate, and cultivate the cares of this world offers us an opportunity to escape. Because we walk by faith and not by sight, we can replace the stimuli many of us are governed by and subject them to a new government, under which Christ has all dominion and authority.

The Bible clearly provides us with instructions on how this is to take place. For this illustration, I will explain this passage of scripture: Take every thought captive (2 Cor. 10:4–6). In this scripture, the prompt is aggressive and not passive. *To take* means to use force to obtain and possess a thing. The second operative word we will look at is the word *captive*. This word implies a forceful action in which a contingency struggle to gain control over whatever thought, idea, concept, behavior, habit, or tendency takes place; it has an established pattern and may govern how one may act or respond to habit, tendency, or thought process. From our new vantage, where we have now either wrote down, listed, or verbally declared out loud what was in control or authority over our lives, we are then instructed to bring them under subjection to the greater authority, which has power to bind up, cast out, and mend whatever was opposing us. The Bible states that all things are subject to the name of Christ. If we now commit to capturing the things which have captured our imaginations and thoughts, by placing these burdens at the feet of Christ, he will, in exchange, give to us a sense of freedom and liberation from the thing which had held us captive.

We *can* disconnect from the world's way of handling phenomena. We can cut ties with these oppressive means, and our ears will be opened to hear faith as we also now learn to speak the things we seek to manifest by declaration. We are no longer governed by our physiological faculties, emotions, feelings, or even our flesh.

Why and how is this possible? Is it simply because Jesus took our place in being he spoiled the flesh, and ultimately his death became the propitiation unto GOD and the price tag for all mankind?

Issues rooted in our flesh are the hardest for us to endure.

Although the flesh is an intimate part of our lives, we must learn to negotiate as we go through this life and not allow our flesh to dominate or manipulate any areas of our lives.

Drugs, alcohol, gambling, sexual issues, money, and possessions are major obstacles to our position to possess our land. Obedience is the posture, and prayer is the prerequisite to receiving the promise. GOD uses our pains to press forth his plans; out of this passion, he presses us into the posterity, but we must assume the posture.

GOD clearly admonishes us about this in his word: "Trust in the LORD with all thine heart, and lean not to thine own understanding, in all thy ways acknowledge Him and he will direct your path."

In hindsight, I can honestly tell you, in my "man-mind," as my wife would say, at times I found myself lost while taking road trips. I could have saved valuable time, energy, gas, and headaches if I would have simply acknowledged that I was lost and needed to ask someone for directions.

In these moments is when I believe we learn some of our greatest life lessons. The simplicity is often covered by the complex way we interpret GOD's messages. The Bible tells us our ways are not his ways, nor our thoughts his, but I'm convinced GOD has a way of depositing his reasoning into our daily existence; the secret, I believe, lies in our patience to take hold of GOD's message "in the moment."

How we take time to meditate on GOD's plan in our day-to-day lives will establish a solid foundation for us to learn how to hear from God—to hear the still small voice that urges us to be still and know he is GOD. More than anything, GOD has orchestrated a divine strategy to usher us into a place of prosperity, but we must adhere to the guidelines he has set. Obedience is the key to abundance; its familiarity is what we know as death.

Our perception makes us see things from the carnal perspective. To the believer, we come to learn that if our minds don't align with GOD's mind, conflict can appear violent and antagonistic, causing us to revere GOD as a dictatorial egomaniac who wants to control our very existence.

Many people draw the line here and choose a life without GOD's love, guidance, or direction. I believe this is where atheists and others draw their lines in the sand and build their platform for the non-existence of GOD; the root of the matter is not wanting to yield to authority but functioning as an agent of selfishness.

Again, GOD clearly admonishes us about this in his word when he says to "trust in the LORD with all thine heart, and lean not to thine own understanding, in all thy ways acknowledge Him and he will direct your path."

In moments like this is when we can develop our character and learn humility. God speaks to us in simple terms to reveal what he desires to work through us; the secret things are given when we simply yield to being taught.

Ironically, this is also the posture in which GOD could release his greatest level of blessing to mankind. In Genesis, it states that Adam "slept." GOD, through the process of removing Adam's rib, multiplied Adam's existence and added beauty, grace, and love to creation by bringing forth Eve.

This phenomenon happened as Adam rested in the garden. Adam did not actively participate, except that he was GOD's first patient! (How is that for cosmetic surgery!) Imagine how much GOD could accomplish in our lives if we'd simply be still and let GOD work on us?

Our bodies, wrapped in our flesh, are a remarkable feat of GOD's engineering; we are designed with intricate systems that are interdependent. Having an imbalance could jeopardize the entire body, thus offsetting not only our own spiritual malfunction but become viral or cancerous, thereby causing more casualties than originally intended.

When an idea, concept, or behavior becomes systemic, it can become lethal. It has to be neutralized, or it can infect not only the body and mind but also the spirit.

The Bible teaches us concepts that relate to reaping and sowing through parables. In parables, Jesus admonishes us about our attitude toward others, giving, humility, and charity. Poor or incorrect attitudes about these concepts can become systemic, thus affecting our harvest. If something affects our harvest, it also affects our ability to sow either naturally or spiritually into others.

When this occurs, balance needs to be restored for the person to become effective.

GOD allows us to experience adversity and challenging situations to inspire us to pursue our God-given destiny the Father GOD has declared over our lives in advance.

We waste time chasing desires that ultimately add no value to our eternal inheritance. God allows even these matters to lead us and guide us into all truth, by causing all things natural and spiritual to work together for the purpose of revealing his glory to all flesh.

Once our flesh receives this revelation, we are made alive in Christ in whom we live, move, and have our being. Aside from Christ, there is no life. Without Jesus (absence from the body), we are dead in trespasses (flesh), hope (faith), for eternity, and absent from the presence of God (spirit).

God desires to draw all souls back into right relationship and give us a place in eternity forever. Here is the irony: our flesh has its own inborn desires. Because of our original patriarchal and matriarchal responses to God's command in the garden, Adam, through the spirit of disobedience, sowed a seed of witchcraft, causing both Adam and Eve to be hidden through their iniquity, which separated them from God.

Contrary to willful disobedience, when we allow God to remove from us hearts of disobedience, selfishness, lust, anger, hatred, jealousy, envy, and dishonesty, we can die to sin. Then we are made alive unto God as we become more conscious of things pertaining to the kingdom (in this world, but not of this world), which allows us to put off the cares and issues of this world (temporal) and seek the (eternal) things which edify God.

God's purposes are not construed upon the same principles as man's, which we identify throughout Scripture. In the Pentateuch, people were killed in mass groups, often because of rebellion, disobedience, and evil acts in the eyes of God. Mass destruction often killed people, children, livestock, and other living things. God would often give specific instructions on what should be done so that no seed of that fallen people would remain.

Often, even the spoils were slaughtered as a sacrifice as well. Blood from living sacrifices brought the remission of sin, that is, it temporarily satisfied the penalty of God's judgment against sin. The priests would make atonement for the people at certain times of the year, offering up dove, goats, lambs, bullocks—offerings to God that were unblemished, perfect specimens; doing so eliminated the need to shed blood ever again, once and for all mankind.

As we realize the significance of this act of love, we become responsible for living not for ourselves but for him, completing the work Christ began during his earthly existence. We become the hands and feet of Jesus. Just as this is to become our nature in Christ, we must learn to die daily.

CHAPTER 6

Nevertheless, Not My Will, but Thy Will Be Done

Life Lesson No. 6
"Undoing the Lazarus effect."

IF WE ARE going to have hope in this life, we must recognize it can't be in our own flesh or in our own abilities. All life is interdependent, but I would rather rely on the source than on the product that comes from it. I don't always need to be right, but I will always need his righteousness.

The information in chapter six helps you complete the process of coming to the end of yourself.

GOD's plan to fulfill his divine will in our humanity is accomplished. This story is further unveiled in the passages of scripture that describe when Jesus is confronted with the news that his friend Lazarus is gravely ill. Lazarus's sisters thought his illness was serious and that he needed immediate attention. Similarly, when we are faced with adversity or problems, we think what we need is GOD's immediate intervention.

Because of our finite understanding as humans, we don't consider that GOD's plan for eternity is being orchestrated. We only know that we need the Almighty's presence to intervene. Thus, the matter which lies at hand causes great unrest in our minds, and consequently, unrest in our spirits and uncertainty in our hearts.

However, GOD is not shaken or disturbed by the events which brings crisis into our humanity. The Bible states that "GOD has known the course our ways afar off." This passage assures us that GOD's eyes are steadfastly watching and witnessing the unfolding of events in our lives.

The only event GOD couldn't bear to watch was the unbearable scourging of his son. The Word states, "He who knew no sin became sin for us" (2 Cor. 5:21). We know Jesus recognized when GOD turned away because he exclaimed, "Father, Father, why has thou forsaken me?" (Matt. 27:46). This same emptiness is what we feel when we are pressed to the point of deathly fear. GOD has given us victory over death and over the fear of death through the altruism of Jesus Christ.

Now let's discuss the final idea of this chapter. To make this message clear, I will call this idea the "undoing of the Lazarus Effect." Because we are humans, and are all sinners, we are in as grave a condition as Lazarus, even though many of us are young, successful, and educated with wealth, prestige, and notoriety.

The relationship forged between mother and baby is an intimate bond. The infant becomes familiar with the rhythmic pattern of the mother in addition to the breathing pattern, the smell of the mother's milk, the sound of the mother's voice, and eventually, the pattern of the mother's response.

Similarly, as newborn babes in Christ, we are dependent on the sincere milk of the word (1 Pet. 2:2) as well as the provisions from our Father even for daily bread. As our relationship continues, others see signs of our growth not in word only but in our deeds.

We may gravitate away from individuals who used to negatively influence our behavior and altogether nix old habits and actions we once enjoyed.

As we mature, our appetites for the things of Christ evolve. Our love and compassion for GOD's people should grow too. We once were selfish; we now are selfless. We once were greedy; now we are generous. Where anger, hatred, and bitterness once grew, we now find joy, love, and compassion. We're constantly being reminded of the indescribable grace that has allowed us to be re-engrafted into the fellowship of his suffering by the shedding of the blood of Jesus Christ. Lazarus was miraculously raised from the dead and restored to his family. The purpose of Lazarus's resurrection was to annul the stigma of death as a final and binding authority over us. Christ, while standing at the tomb, wept and prayed, but then commanded the bystanders to remove the stone. This was significant because death represented "an unbearable weight which we cannot endure nor remove of our own accord." Jesus purposely arrived purposely four days after Lazarus's untimely death to demonstrate to the believers that hope of life eternal and power over the grave are real; however, to unbelievers, the message was quite different. Jesus demonstrated compassion for the lost souls of humanity; because of this work, many unbelievers decided to follow Christ and believed him to be the Son of GOD.

By claiming to be "the resurrection," Jesus shows us that GOD has a plan that extends beyond our temporal existence. The closer we matriculate toward his plan, the less our mortality plays a role in this present world.

GOD's ultimate plan has more value toward our eternal existence.

The effect we should be aware of is "becoming dead again." Shall we continue in sin that grace may abound? GOD forbid! We must resist the desire to go back into our grave clothes and bondages, which are meant to suspend our growth. GOD wants us to stand fast in the liberty which made us free. In liberty, captives are set free, those who are ensnared are loosed, and the eyes of those who are blind are opened. In liberty, we know that death to us is life in GOD, as we allow the resurrection of Christ to cause us to live more abundantly. Life in GOD is the only way we preserve and display the love of God effectively.

Finally, we must be willing to sacrifice for others the way Jesus sacrificed his life for us. Our sacrifice must serve a greater purpose than meeting our own selfish desires. We display the altruistic nature of Christ and the ultimate hope of glory when we do as Christ does. Each of us will have to either acknowledge or deny the person of

Jesus Christ before we die. Our response will determine whether Christ will deny or proclaim us before the Father.

We must recognize we are flawed and admit we need to be restored to Christ. Like any great artist, painter, or curator, Jesus, the masterful artisan, revives the beauty in each of his creations, bringing forth its maximum value, beauty, purpose, and splendor.

To the untrained eye, each creation (person) may display only some potential and, if any, very little value to the one who beholds the uniqueness of these works. However, to the master artisan, the masterpiece is merely covered by the obscurity of its unfulfilled potential, whether it needs to be cut, carved, etched, painted, drawn, refined, sketched or proofed. Only the master knows what process each needs to go through to reveal its greatest value to the universe.

The process may require adding, extracting, increasing, diminishing, reforming, hardening, or softening, but the end product reveals not only the creation but also the creator's genius and thoughts toward his creation in his plan.

Here is an example of this: God's plan to raise Lazarus from the grave foreshadowed Jesus's purpose to redeem all mankind and reconcile the relationship of man back to fellowship with God. Likewise, we all have been given "life assignments" to redeem/reconcile whatever issues we face. As we go through life, we demonstrate God's faithfulness to love us beyond our frail attempts to understand the boundless measures of our eternal paramour.

The faith of Lazarus's two sisters represents the parallel of how the world perceives faith. Martha represents most people—superficial believers who embrace some vague concept of GOD by proxy. GOD is a concept that represents order and tradition based on religious values, customs, culture, and ideologies of a vague, vain sense of a servant-master relationship. Thus, her relationship is based on ritualism and obscurity. In this relationship, GOD is far and not near. Although Martha was fortunate to know Christ in proximity, she still felt that GOD was distant and not intimately connected to their lives. Mary, on the other hand, represents believers who have chosen the greater posture to serve and draw nigh to the Lord. Mary understood that Christ was the embodiment of GOD's intimacy; He came to experience our human condition and suffering, but with the authority to offer a more excellent way by his example of resisting temptation, all while demonstrating compassion for our shortcomings.

This was paramount when she approached Christ about the condition of her brother Lazarus. The posture of humility Mary demonstrated became the catalyst for Christ, who intervened. When Martha approached Christ, he responded based on her religious mind; when Mary approached him, his response was motivated by her faithful heart.

Both of their approaches moved Jesus, but Mary's position of hope touched Christ and activated a response because of her faith in GOD.

Her response undid the effect of Lazarus's condition, which resulted in him arising from the grave.

We have been given a charge to provoke GOD to "unveil his will on earth, as he does in heaven" (Matt. 6:10). Our earthly duty is to fulfill the Lord's glory by reverence, which is often referred to as *fear*, or *to pay meticulous attention to*.

We are reminded that our very existence is based on this principle. Our ability to adhere to the logos and decree the *ruach*, or "breath of life," will determine and bring either justification of how we live, or condemnation for why we didn't choose to live abundantly in the presence of Almighty GOD.

When GOD realizes our posture of humility, it provokes him to go beyond the reasonable expectation and alter others' expectations to choose his good pleasure. Simply put, GOD is moved to take action on behalf of the believer who demonstrates his work of faith and perseverance despite the overwhelming obstacles and challenges our lives present (Heb. 11:6).

The currency of heaven is faith; this is the wealth of the believers on earth. We know this because the Bible tells us the earth was framed by it, Christ was raised because of it, and Abraham was counted as righteous because he had it. Moreover, a measure of it was given to each one of us. Mary had great faith to compel Jesus to undo what bound Lazarus and to call him from death to life.

We have been trained from childhood to constantly revert to our old tendencies. We are told to conform to societal norms, warned against challenging the status quo, and expected to never question authority. Strongholds like these keep us bound. The longer we are bound, the more comfortable the constraints become; in the end, they entangle us until escape isn't possible. Christ has called us to not again be intertwined in things that result in our bondage. I encourage you to break free from your fears, shame, and doubts and live more abundantly. Your testimony could be someone else's deliverance message!

CHAPTER 7

Behold, I Make All Things New

Life Lesson No. 7
"Perfect doesn't mean flawless; it means mature."

FOR SEVERAL YEARS of my life, I lived beneath my privileges. I thought I needed to be a model child, a model student, and a sinless Christian, among a myriad of other stereotypes I subscribed to about myself and the world. During these times, even though I sought hard to please and meet the expectations of so many others, I forgot myself. I often felt pressured to overachieve just to find satisfaction in who I was. Imagine it: I worked hard to measure up to others who didn't work as hard at it.

The overachiever zone—that's where I found myself—sometimes feeling pretentious and even prideful. I felt like I had to "one-up" people and compare my accomplishments to theirs. This went on throughout my school years. I met my first obstacle in college, not because of the work, but because of the philosophical understanding of perfection.

I remember being challenged by my philosophy professor on basic ideals of how we perceived the world around us.

One lesson dealt with the essence of beauty. I, being an overachiever, used my biblical knowledge to answer the question "What is beauty?" because I came across this scripture in Ecclesiastes 3:11: "He has made everything beautiful in his time: and he has set the world in their heart so that no man can find out the work that God has made from the beginning." I concluded that beauty is everything, but through some form of metamorphosis, it can indeed be lost.

I further examined myself through the lens of the God who created me, determined that beauty can also go through stages from one level to the next as it matures/perfects, that is, the transformation process of wine, which is, by the way, where the term "perfect" comes from.

Through this lesson, I learned God has made each of us uniquely beautiful. It is then our responsibility to develop, mature, and refine the manner in which we perfect to display the finished product of his excellent craftsmanship, which he has invested in each one of his creations—including you.

In this final chapter, I was challenged with several situations that forced me to ask myself about what I believe.

Do I believe in GOD of the scriptures, or do I believe that GOD is one who is limited by "the cares of this world"?

How many times have we given GOD our human expectations and relied on our understanding to explain how GOD should respond to the trials and tribulations we are all destined to encounter?

I conclude that GOD intervenes in our lives in a realm of sovereignty incomprehensible to us.

When I accepted that I have this, I yielded my expectation to one of hope rooted in the confidence that our GOD owes no explanation for when, why, how, or if he chooses to visit us with the realm of dominion power. The physics of our world are not in any way a factor when GOD, in his power, decides to express his authority in a way we describe as miraculous. Where he dwells, all things fully await his bidding as Creator and sovereign Lord; He makes all things new.

The miraculous is a phenomena within our earthly realm that is beyond human logic, rationale, or any scientific method of explanation. Simply put, things may happen without a practical explanation.

Conversely, in the realm where GOD reigns, miracles are common. It's because where he dwells, all things are possible in his omnipotence. Miracles are commonplace in the presence of God.

As believers, we are encouraged to create an environment conducive to producing "signs and wonders that will follow the ones who believe." We are responsible for living a life that allows God to demonstrate his power in our lives as well as in the lives of others.

In this chapter, I will describe how my faith was restored in God and the miraculous event I witnessed firsthand.

The event was inexplicable and beyond understanding. To an outsider, it may even appear to be fabricated or exaggerated.

However, I assure you that I personally witnessed all of the events I am about to describe. How powerful and mysterious God is!

These experiences strengthened my beliefs and validated my faith. I *know* God functions and manifests his power through events that demonstrate supernatural powers to enhance our lives and even affect our natural realm with power to change not only our physical lives, but challenge our faith in him.

In 1998, I was privileged to work as a caseworker with an agency that serves individuals who have AIDS and HIV in the Dallas, Texas, area.

I remember when I met "Adam" (name changed to protect privacy). He was a young (in his early 30s) African American who became infected while having sexual relationships with both males and females. When we met, his health had deteriorated to full-blown AIDS (medically, less than two hundred T cells), and he was gravely ill.

Adam took female hormones, retrovirals, nucleotides, and other HIV antivirals and cocktails (over one hundred pills, at about $1100 in value) and was experiencing feminine outgrowths, less facial hair growth, and voice change. He carried all of his medications in a brown paper bag from Peabody Clinic.

Because of the disease, he looked much older than he was. He came into our office to request bus passes and housing assistance through HOPWA (Housing Opportunities for Persons with AIDS), but we couldn't help him at that time because he wasn't a primary client of our agency. After I interviewed him during a brief qualification session, I found financial resources for him through one of our new programs. I explained to him that we would need to complete a comprehensive case management session to get him enrolled, to which he agreed. I remember thinking that this may be an opportunity to reach him at a deeper level and to inspire him through hope. That day is when I found out why he remained somber and looked bleak. When we first talked, he was reserved; however, as we continued our conversation, he began to share more about his journey and how he became infected. (To protect his privacy, I will not disclose details about his journey.) Through my position, I had access to patient records, which also listed out illnesses patients had that were caused by those diseases. Adam shared his medical records with me. Although I understood the severity of his prognosis according to medical terminology, I knew that spiritually, he was about to have a Saul-on-Damascus-Road experience.

Now, before I continue telling you about Adam, I want to share what I was going through when we crossed paths. You see, I was on my own soul-searching journey. I had recently asked God to "heal my unbelief." I, much like many other people during the time in the late 90s, was inundated with the overwhelming toll of AIDS and HIV. During that time until about 2016, twenty-three million people worldwide died as a result of AIDS and HIV-related illnesses. It seemed like every time you turned on any media outlet, a new report about the spread of these diseases was the topic. We were inundated with information and pandemic-focused reports from around the world about the seemingly relentless spread of this virus, which affected millions of people. In my prayers, I would constantly declare this to God: "Father, I know you are able to do anything, but I desire to see the miraculous." Little did I know that God was working a miracle that I would witness *and* also participate in through activation.

Here's what happened. While Adam talked to me about his journey, I began to feel empathy I couldn't fully explain. It was as if I was put in his position, not physically but spiritually. I felt an obligation to help him reconcile some of his past hurts. Galatians 6:1 states if you find a brother in a fault, to restore such a one. This in no way excuses him from his obligation, but it does provide him a means to see himself as beloved of God and gives him grace to repent.

I felt compelled to say these words to Adam: I offered him an apology on behalf of others who mistreated him from his church; these people wrongly ostracized him and exploited him to justify their own self-righteousness. I also asked him to forgive me, on behalf of his family members who he had not forgiven. The Holy Spirit gave me this revelation, and I obeyed. Finally, before Adam asked me to pray for him, I asked him to take a moment and forgive himself for all of his own self-depraving, self-destructive behaviors he committed against himself. The Bible instructs us to forgive and reconcile with those who we have ought with, and then if we expect God to answer then to pray (Matt. 5:23–24).

Instinctively, I followed this protocol, and I was given specific instructions on how to pray for this man. I asked Adam if he believed in miracles. He reluctantly said, "No," but then added, "I have been to church, and I believe in God, but not in too many preachers."

He concluded by saying he had never felt God's power. After I prayed for him, he said he felt a surge of energy moving through his body, and he felt cold, and then hot." I simply said, "I believe for you," and this phenomenon went on for about forty-five minutes while he sobbed inconsolably.

Regardless of what he believed, I truly expected him to experience God's power in person and to receive some form of God's manifestation for the condition which he has experienced. When we confront issues in life with unconditional love, which is the greatest power in the whole earth, one can rely on the intervention of God, because the environment God can expand his presence into is one that demonstrates love.

The new command that Jesus gave was to "love one another as I have loved you and that you also love one another" (John 13:34).

If there is one thing that is needed in our world, it is an environment of love, whereby God can dwell and do the miraculous among his people.

After some time, Adam arose from the floor. He gathered himself and said he felt energy flowing and also felt very upbeat.

Adam was elated and said, "I believe I am healed." He responded by taking the brown paper bag full of medications and dropping it into the trash can!

Keep in mind this is the medication doctors claimed was keeping him alive, and at the time, he was gravely ill.

Almost four months later, when I had nearly forgotten the incident, Adam showed up at our office again. This time, though, I didn't recognize who he was! His appearance was completely changed from what he looked like months ago. I remembered a frail man who looked as if he was facing dire circumstances; the man standing in front of me did not have that appearance. He looked vibrant, alive, and strong. He had regained weight, his face was restored to normal, and he didn't look sickly. To say the least, I was stunned and shocked—I did not know who he was until he told me! After a few minutes being dumbstruck, I followed Adam back to one of the conference rooms at his request. He said he wanted to show me something in private.

We went into the room, and I ensured him that we were in a secured environment. He pulled out his checkup paperwork and handed it to me. I had previously read this type of record before from other clients. I understood the two things we should look for: the viral load and the T cell count. Adam's medical records were remarkable, considering the last time I saw him. He could have literally died of any "opportunistic infection" based on his previous prognosis. That day, I read an official report he had just received from his doctor, which read, "T cell count <1100 and viral load undetectable"! After I gathered myself, I realized I was looking at a miracle!

Immediately, a feeling of euphoria enveloped my whole body. I had no words or audible expression, but felt a great sense of awe.

Adam sat there silently wiping away tears. He looked at me and said, "You are a true man of God."

I felt like there was a revelation of God's miraculous works released. In fact, I felt that I was ready to challenge anything that I might face.

More than that, I felt God had truly visited this individual. What some may perceive as a dire and desperate situation was the perfect environment for God to exhibit the miraculous.

Since this incident, I have sought out opportunities to display God's love and establish an environment where he can do works in the supernatural.

I would have to write many more chapters to share with you other examples of God's healing virtue I have seen take place in the lives of others. Over the years, I have seen a myriad of phenomena which some might consider miraculous: many were healing of the body, others were of the spirit, and some also involved natural matters.

Thus, I encourage you to always create environments whereby God can have room in your daily life to invade your natural existence with his supernatural activity. Part of our responsibility as believers is to create a sustainable environment for God to inhabit our world, as evidenced in the Lord's Prayer. It starts out with these words: "Our Father, which art in heaven; hallowed be thy Name, thy kingdom come, thy will be done on earth as it is in heaven."

The will of God states we should prosper and live in good health as we grow in spiritual understanding (soul prosperity).

I pray the events and matters addressed in this book will enlighten your spiritual understanding and cause you to increase in health and wisdom in the knowledge of God, his Son Christ, and the workings of the Holy Spirit in your life. We must learn that knowledge (information), which enlightens our understanding but doesn't enhance our spiritual growth and development, becomes revelation or provides us with a practical or personal way to use what we've learned (application) as will cause us to live in stagnation. God always desires for us to accelerate in (elevation) (enhance, advance) our socio-emotional spiritual growth.

For us to fully activate our lives into our destiny and function in our purpose, the old nature of the character, our humanity, must die.

Everything in our natural energy resists our God-nature due to sin (Gen. 3:15).

Christ came that we might have life, and have it more abundantly in our day-to-day life. Abundant life includes a life of miracles.

We often resist what we don't understand, especially if it goes against our natural tendencies or inclinations. Life has a way of providing us with situations that will challenge us to rise up or resist the moment. God is constantly beckoning us to rise to the occasion of displaying his glory through our daily lives. True abundance is in seeing steps that lead us to accomplish far more than what we expect we can achieve; the results exceed what we believed was even possible.

As you learn to build yourself up in the faith of God, you will develop an "abundance mentality." This is a supernatural expectation that grows as we acknowledge our fragile human abilities. In light of this, God honors our sincere honesty to recognize where our strength diminishes and his begins. Thus, our expectations are tempered in our strength and given room to become whatever God has planned for them to become in his divine will.

Learning where to yield to God's will can prevent a lot of unnecessary struggle and conflict we experience. God seeks our obedience to allow us to maximize his ability to demonstrate the spirit of his might.

This will be a lifelong lesson that you will have ample opportunities to practice and learn as you grow.

Your greatest fight will be to keep your flesh under subjection, which again is contrary to our humanity. We are spirit beings who are housed in a physical environment; the natural proclivity will be to respond in the capacity that dominates our experience. The average person has more than twenty pounds of skin to cover his or her body; in fact, the skin, or flesh, is the largest single organ of the body. It stands to reason that our flesh would be what is most susceptible to our sin nature, because it is the most exposed.

I am beyond convinced that you will have to place your flesh under subjection to overcome the sensual desire to respond to its constant need for being acknowledged. When a person no longer feels the need to address what the flesh wants, he or she is ready for the next level of transformation or transition. That person no longer has need for external stimuli, which can hinder the ability to overcome the process of becoming a new creation. God, in his infinite wisdom, knows what experiences to give us and the life journey we need to take so that we develop the nature he desires for us as we renew our minds.

It is my prayer that you not only read this book and apply the lessons and techniques mentioned but also realize that no flesh can glory in God's presence. No one has seen God and lived, but they who worship the Lord must worship him in Spirit and Truth.

Would you share this book with someone who is in the valley of decision in their life? Let that person know the transformational power of the Most High God will give life, and life more abundantly.

Father, in the name of Jesus Christ, may the readers who partake of the lessons and the wisdom which you have imparted to me in this book become salt and light to the people around them. Let your words through me not only encourage their spiritual development but increase their faith in knowing that you are an ever-present God who desires to have a relationship with us as we submit to knowing you through the Word and the fellowship of sufferings, which work to strengthen our faith and fortify our understanding. I pray that these readers will vow to strive to trust you with the intimate details of their lives by confessing their weaknesses and allowing you to cover them as they continue to dwell in the secret place of the Most High. I pray they will abide under your shadow in power, love, and a sound mind as they learn that in patience, they will possess their souls. Finally, I pray that you will use them to do mighty and excellent exploits for the kingdom in the years to come, in the excellency of your power, as they learn to die in your presence that they might live the abundant life the you have promised as an inheritance to them who choose to walk upright before you. In Jesus's name. Amen!

Be blessed, be empowered, be encouraged.

ABOUT THE AUTHOR

 PATRICK PARKER IS a neophyte author who draws from his experience and twenty-four years of ministry as an evangelist, who hosted a local TV show in Dallas, *Shifting the Atmosphere with FIRE Ministries*, who has experienced both the highs and lows of the Christian experience, shares from the perspective of his challenging but inspiring relationship in getting to know God through his own personal triumphs and heart-wrenching failures. Patrick is currently married nineteen years, with three children, and expands on his perspective of the vanishing core doctrines of Christian faith. This book chronicles ideas which have been hot-button topics and subjects of debate for both Christians and non-Christians alike, but provide perspectives that give insight and relevance to why many have not found Christianity as appealing as it was during the late twentieth century. As a former member of the US Air Force and diligent seeker of the truth, Patrick shares insightful revelations from his personal life experiences which brings him face-to-face with the revelation that GOD has controlled his destiny, and he has been mandated to "make an impact and not just and impression" to inspire all who chance to read the work which culminates in seven chapters which cultivate the cerebral levels of spiritual thought.

CPSIA information can be obtained
at www.ICGtesting.com
Printed in the USA
LVHW031203100221
678885LV00004BA/799